# The Prayers of Namaste

## My Thanks

To my family, friends and supporters for their love, prayers and good wishes.

You have kept me moving forward.

To My husband Vincent, your help has been invaluable in bringing this book to my readers.

## Acknowledgement

To Robert D. Spaeth Images for the cover photograph.

Rob's talented eye and open heart are a beautiful gift that I am very grateful for.

# Table of Contents

"Just a Reminder,

In case you forgot,

In case you thought otherwise,

Or in case you never knew…

There is nothing you can't have

There is nothing you can't do

There is nothing you can't be.

Okay?"

*Notes from the Universe*

by Mike Dooley

# Introduction

Dear Reader,

I was asked by so many of you who read my first book, *Believe, A Journey of Enlightenment*, to please create a separate book of prayers from the prayers given within that book. This book was created for all of you.

I have entitled it "The Prayers of Namaste" because the word "Namaste" in the Sanskrit language means; that which is in me recognizes and honors that which is in you. I am you and you are me and we are one.

In Sanskrit "Namaste" is a gesture of greeting, and represents the deep belief that each of us carries within us a divine spark, which resides within each and every one of our heart centers. It is this divine spark that recognizes and acknowledges the same divine spark radiating from the heart center of every human being. Namaste is used as a bow of greeting or farewell, and is made by holding the hands pressed together, palm to palm, at the center of the chest in front of the heart center, with the eyes closed and the head bowed in respect one to the other. "Namaste" can also be expressed by placing the hands pressed together in front of the brow, or third eye, located in the middle of the forehead, bowing the head and then bringing the hands down to the level of the heart. This form of "Namaste" is an especially deep form of respect shown one to the other, in acknowledgement from the soul in one to the soul in another.

Yet, to fully understand the connotation behind the power of this sacred Sanskrit word one must also understand the meaning held within the word itself, as the truth behind all words can be found hidden within every language expressed upon this planet. In Sanskrit the word Namaste translates as follows; "Nama" means to bow, "A" means "I", and "Te" means "You". Therefore the word "Namaste" literally translates; "Bow Me You" or "I Bow to you" and is phonetically pronounced as "Nah-Mah-Stay".

It is within this simple yet beautiful act of respect that the intellect of the mind then merges with the power of the heart, creating a bridge of light linking one to the other and opening up the window to the soul. Namaste creates a universal connection of spiritual power as it bridges and crosses all divides of creed, gender and belief systems. Such is the power behind this one sacred word. For you see, the body's mind, heart and soul are not separate but intrinsically linked one to the other, and together form one single voice of power. It is within this voice when expressed through the power of mantra or prayer, held within the equally powerful vehicle of meditation, that we create a bridge of light integrating all parts of ourselves into the whole and become one voice, one expression and one single heartbeat. When we begin to embrace the many varying tools embracing mantras, prayers and meditations, which essentially are all vehicles of light, and use these forms of expression to invoke good into our lives, our voices when raised in prayer or chant then become powerful tools of transformation. This enables us to expand ourselves out of linear confinement into the realm of unlimited possibility and potential, and become more than we ever thought it was possible to become.

Prayer and meditation combine and integrate the heart with the intellect through the powerful vehicle of the breath, or "Prana", as the breath is the body's tool of total awareness as well as of transformation. It is only through the manipulation of the breath that one can achieve the greatest of all mind and body changes. In Yoga there is a 1:1 ratio in regards to the breath wherein inhale and exhale are of equal proportions. When this ratio is achieved the body will literally warm up. When the exhaled breath is longer then the inhaled breath, on the other hand, the body will then begin to cool down. In Yoga this is referred to as a 1:2 ratio. The longer the ratios of exhale to inhale are, the calmer the nervous system becomes. This is how powerful the breath is. When calm is achieved through the breath, it is referred to in Yoga philosophy as "Victorious Breath".

The position of the body in meditation in regards to the breath is important, as you want to make sure your chakra system which comprises the seven energy centers that align you from within are fully lined up so that the energy in the body flows freely. These chakra centers of light and frequency are located in a vertical line up and down your spine, and are anchored within the etheric body which governs the flow of energy to all four of your body's systems. This system is comprised of the Physical, Emotional, Mental, and Spiritual bodies often referred to as "PEMS".

Within each of your chakras resides a seat of consciousness represented by all of the emotions that are held there. These seats of consciousness play a crucial role in our body's ability to heal itself as when the emotions held within these energy centers are in balance and alignment ... so too are we. Within prayer or meditation these chakras can be brought        into        complete alignment, which in turn can bring complete balance to your entire being. Therefore sitting in a comfortable position with the spine, neck and head erect is much more effective than sitting slumped. This allows the energy to flow freely rather than stagnating and becoming blocked, which defeats the purpose of the exercise. When you sit with your feet flat on the ground in a comfortable chair or in a lotus position with pillows behind you keeping your spine and head erect and begin to take slow and even breaths, in and out rhythmically, your body will naturally settle into a relaxed state which is at the same time both calming as well as soothing. As you achieve this state, open yourself up to receive whatever it is the universe wants to send you, and let the energy moving into you just flow unobstructed. This is where if you are so inclined, you can offer up either a prayer or mantra, which when either silently or verbally spoken, will vibrate and resonate within you connecting your energy to the universal energy and source of all things. This amazing energy source is available to all of us just for the asking. It is important to understand that there is no one way to meditate, and each way will be as unique as the one embracing it. When you close your eyes and move into rhythmic breath and surrender self to the breath, all of your bodies comprising both your subtle and physical anatomy will begin to move into synchronistic harmony with each other and merge together as one. This single act of surrendering self to the breath during meditation is what has the power to lead you down the pathway to total transformation. This simple process can then become a powerful tool that when embraced and used daily has the potential to open the door through which the mind and the heart interface, synchronize, and merge into one powerful vehicle of expression.

When beginning the process of meditation I always take three deep and even breaths of awareness as I begin the process of connecting myself with my Guides and the source of all things. As I do, I begin to enter into a deep meditative state, and it is only within this state of being that the heart and the intellect have the power to merge and become one. As you inhale through the nose deeply and without strain your lungs will begin to fill up with the breath of life. As you retain and hold that breath inside of you with full awareness for as long as possible, again without strain, you will then begin the process of spiritual integration. Within Yoga philosophy this process is referred to as "Antarkumbhaka" which simply means inner retention. As we accomplish this process of spiritual integration our bodies will begin to take on a lightness of being. For some their bodies will actually begin to feel lighter. Then as we exhale fully and slowly out through the mouth until both our lungs and our abdomen are empty of breath, and retain and hold the breath outside the body with full awareness for as long as possible, again without strain, we then begin to master the prana or breath of life which is our energy and vital life force. This life force and Divine energy dwells within us, as us. Within Sanskrit and Yoga philosophies this process is referred to as "Bahya Kumbhaka", which is the cessation of breath when exhaling is complete. This is known as "outer breath retention" and when controlled without strain to the body can bring both the subtle and physical anatomy into alignment, as when one controls the breath, one "controls everything". It is during this stage of meditation that it becomes equally important "to listen" to the sound of your breath. As you begin to listen to the breath, you will slowly begin to move into alignment with it and become one with it. As you move into alignment, the rhythm of the breath begins to take on a musical cadence all

5

of its own, which will be as different and as unique as the one experiencing it. Each person will have their own personal rhythm, and through the rhythm of the breath will begin to create and experience their own symphony of expression. If you let it, this can open up portals of enlightenment creating a spiritual awakening from within. This expression of breath then becomes each person's unique and very personal thumbprint of spiritual identity. So, the mastering of the breath during meditation becomes one of our greatest tools in life. As we move into synchronistic rhythm with our breath and do so for at least 15 minutes a day, at the end of one month our bodies will have begun the process of total transformation. This total transformation begins to occur during daily meditation due to the fact that the breath controls all of the body's vital signs. The mastering of the breath has the power to lower tension and anxiety within the physical body which when left to run amok can create a slew of problems within the many different systems of our body all on their own. Thus it follows that if tension and anxiety are controlled or eliminated the body, quite simply put, will move back into balance and alignment. For each of us our transformation truly begins with the innate ability each of us has to go within and invoke our inner power. As we achieve this inner power and begin to learn to control the rhythm of our breath during meditation we create a doorway we each walk through to achieve the spiritual integration of our souls. When the energy within us connects with the spiritual energy of creation, we have the power to ignite our inner light and illuminate not only ourselves but the entire planet as well.

In order to achieve perfect breath it is so important that we begin to understand that the breath truly controls all of the biological systems and functions of the body. As such, when we experience any form of agitation we can actually begin to transform that agitation simply by taking slow and deep breaths in and out within the 1:2 ratio, which quickly will begin to put our bodies into a state of calmness. Equally, when we do not choose to control our breaths during times of elevated agitation and our breathing begins to spiral out of control becoming erratic and accelerated, our bodies will begin to hyperventilate, which will then begin to put us into a state of panic. Such is the power the breath has over every aspect of our beings.

A while ago while on vacation with my husband and driving into New York City to have lunch with a friend, I began to get carsick due to stop and go traffic. It was only by quickly controlling my breathing and taking deep even breaths in and out in a 1:2 ratio that I was able to bring myself out of queasiness and back into balance and into a state of calmness. On that day I finally began to comprehend just how powerful the process of controlling the breath was to the well-being of the body. You see, when we focus our intent on the breath and give it our complete concentration as I did that day, we automatically begin the process of calming our bodies down and moving them out of agitation and back into balance. This process of interfacing the breath within all of the systems within the body has the potential to cure us of every disease we have ever embraced through negative thought patterns. If we embrace negativity, that deteriorates us faster than anything we could ever imagine, and it is this key of negativity that opens the lock to all diseases known to mankind. When the interface between the breath and the systems within the human body occurs, it quickly begins to bring changes within the biological structure, and subtly begins to create a shift within the body's infrastructure that can usher in a state of wellbeing and balance. This is why, as I stated earlier, practicing daily meditation through the powerful vehicle of the breath can at the end of just one month begin to totally transform the infrastructure of our bodies. Now, begin to imagine just how many diseases and illnesses could be eradicated by simply learning to harness the power of the breath!

When we finally begin to understand, embrace and acknowledge our individual powers and harness those powers within the parameters of positive thought and gratitude, fully expressed during meditation, we not only elevate our own spiritual vibrations, but collectively begin to change the vibrations of the entire planet as well, as we are all connected and are all one. This process of meditative prayer and the embracement of "Namaste" then becomes a global extension of our collective spiritual evolution, and it is only through this process that we can collectively begin to achieve world peace.

The prayers and mantras given within this book, as well as any prayers or mantras you embrace, can help you begin your own personal journey of enlightenment. Prayers and mantras have the power to help you connect your heart with your intellect, creating a bridge of awareness that the mind can then travel upon. This journey can, if you allow it, begin to transform your state of awareness and set you upon a pathway where all questions are answered and all answers are understood.

So I give to you these mantras and prayers to use as a tool of light in order to help you unlock the mysteries of the heart and open up the pathway of discovery, through which the mind is then released from its limitation and set free into a realm of unlimited possibilities and potentials. Here, the probable outcomes are endless, the possibilities infinite, and the potential for enlightenment is oh, so powerful!

As each of you begins to acknowledge and embrace your inner light and begins to radiate that light out into the world, you begin to weaken the pathway that negativity travels upon. The collective expression of light which travels upon the higher frequency of love effectively decreases the food supply that negativity feeds upon, as all negativity feeds off of anger, hatred, and chaos as well as all emotions related to fear. When this pathway of light is activated through the use of either prayers and/or mantras, it expands within the heart and then moves into the mind creating a powerful synergy of light that then radiates out of the mind to interface with all of the light projected throughout this beautiful planet. This is how powerful this light activation is. Once you activate, acknowledge and expand this light within you, it is then yours to harness and use. Light simply eradicates and eliminates negativity's ability to contaminate the soul. So hold the light within you and become the highest expression of yourselves, always remembering that the light in me sees and honors the same light which dwells within you... Always... "Namaste"


*Darkness cannot drive out darkness; only light can do that.*
Martin Luther King, Jr.

"Did you realize that whenever you gave anything, to anyone, you gave to the entire world?

And did you realize that for every path you've walked, for every stone you've turned over, and for every door you've knocked on, you did so for everyone?

And finally, did you realize that whenever you felt love, for any reason whatsoever, you irrevocably lifted the entire planet higher into the light?

Thanks from all of us."

*Notes from the Universe*
by Mike Dooley

# Tools for Transformation

Each of us holds within us a tremendous power that is our greatest tool for manifestation and ultimately for complete transformation. This is the inner power each of us has that enables us to visualize and imagine whatever it is we desire to create right down to its most minute details. When we hold that vision within our minds and give it our complete focus and concentration and then infuse that vision with the emotion of gratitude, we then bring it into our realities and begin to experience it in our lives. You see, when we imagine ourselves having something and then imagine how we would feel upon receiving it, the Universe kicks into high gear and gives us exactly what we want. As you begin to imagine and create your dreams and your realities, it is important that you are very careful and very clear about what you wish for, because you may be thinking negative thoughts and thus put the power of emotion behind those thoughts. Whatever thoughts you are giving your focus to will manifest into your lives, as the Universe does not discriminate between good or bad, it simply gives us whatever we desire to experience.

This process of manifesting our realities is called creative visualization and it is one of the most powerful tools behind the Law of Abundance. If we want to have an abundant life we have to understand the power that lies behind this tool and use it to manifest and create the lives we wish to experience. All highly successful people completely understand how to harness the amazing power that lies behind this tool and use it daily to manifest and co-create their dreams, bringing into their realities exactly what it is they wish to experience. The techniques used within Creative Visualization are made effective and put into motion whenever we use our imaginations to create whatever it is we wish to experience. It is somewhat similar to the game of "Make Believe" we all played when we were children where we imagined how we wanted to live, the kind of house we would someday buy, and even the families we would one day have, only now we are not just dreaming it but are also giving it both our focus and our intent. The only difference between the two is in the deep inner knowledge that what we are now imagining and focusing on, and infusing with an attitude of gratitude, will manifest for us and become our realities.

As you begin to imagine a different reality and do so with intent and conviction, your thoughts then create a powerful vortex of energy that moves out into the Universe to be received, filled and then sent back to you to experience. It is just that simple. It is really all about intent and focus, as whatever your intent and focus are will be exactly what you bring into your lives to experience.

As you begin to embrace this concept have a little fun with it. Begin to play around with it. Maybe begin by imagining a parking space opening up for you right where you need it to be. This is a really easy and basic type of manifestation that is fun to do. Or try imagining whatever it is you need to purchase being right in front of you as soon as you enter the store. Believe me, these simple and easy methods of creative visualization can make your lives a whole lot easier, and as they begin to manifest for you they will also become a lot of fun to play around with as well! As you get the hang of it you can move into more complicated manifestations like manifesting money when you need it. Maybe you have bills to pay and no way to pay them and out of the blue a refund check comes in the mail giving you exactly what you need, or maybe you find yourself walking through a parking lot and look down and find the perfect amount of money you need at exactly the right moment! Another great way to manifest your reality, especially if you are in sales and are trying to make your quota, is to imagine the end result before you actually begin your year. All great athletes imagine winning the game even before the game begins. Once you get the hang of this the rest will take care of itself. Don't focus on how the abundance you are imagining will come but rather be expansive and just send the thought out into the universe for the Universe to fill. In other words don't get caught up in who will give you what you want, rather just put it out there and know your order will be received and sent back to you. Open up to the possibilities of magic and magic will manifest for you. You see, there is nothing you cannot create when you use the power of the mind. So stop focusing on what is not working for you, let it go, release it to the universe and begin to change your focus to what will work for you. This will begin to change the electrical frequency vibrations that your dreams travel upon, with the potential to usher into your lives amazing abundance. Quite simply put, by focusing on what is working for you it keeps a positive vibration going and changes the frequency of your thoughts to a much higher band of vibrational frequency. It is really just that simple.

During this process, having an attitude of gratitude is very important, as gratitude is the engine that drives the many different facets of the Law of Abundance; from the Law of Creative Visualization, to the Law of Attraction, to the Law of Deliberate Creation. Having an attitude of gratitude creates a pathway of light, which allows even more abundance to manifest into your lives. As we embrace gratitude and give Thanks for what we have, we open our arms to receive even more. Saying, "Thank You", with gratitude simply brings more good experiences your way and deepens the hue and color of your lives. Gratitude changes the parameters of your realities and broadens the horizons of your dreams. It raises your vibrations, which in turn sets the tone that your mind then creates upon. It is this process which allows the mind and the intellect to interface with the heart embracing the higher vibrational frequency energies of Love. This love energy travels faster than the speed of light and is the single most powerful energy in creation. When this interface occurs it has the potential to remove all roadblocks and restrictions that we have created through our embracement of negativity. This powerful force behind gratitude is simply amazing! You see, when we embrace gratitude and unconditional love and hold them within us they begin to change the tone of the neurotransmitters in our brain allowing the mind and the intellect to synchronize into one mighty force of transformation.

When we awaken every morning it is important to embrace a sense of gratitude for the day and everything around us. When we give each new day our blessing and our joy we then set the frequency tone for that day. This ushers into our presence more joy and more blessings, now... how cool is that! As soon your head comes off the pillow try giving thanks for "everything". Look around you and have a profound sense of gratitude for all of the beauty Mother Nature has to offer. It is within this moment every day that I give gratitude for life! This not only sets the tone for my day but it also uplifts my spirit and gives me a deep sense of wellbeing. You will, as you get the hang of this, get better at controlling the tone and cadence of each new day, and as you begin to see the amazing results this brings to you, it will become as natural for you as breathing. So let giving thanks for everything in your life and for all that you have be your first conscious thought every morning, and then sit back and watch magic begin to manifest into your realities. Watch the texture of your lives begin to change before your eyes. For when you embrace this transforming emotion of gratitude, you begin to recreate your matrix. You change your reality from what was, to what it is now not only possible but also probable to become. As the process begins to transform your lives you will begin to realize the depth and scope of your own powers and potential, because as you are transformed, everything around you is transformed as well; those you love, those you come into contact with, are all affected by your vibrational shift.

When we finally begin to understand the deep changes that having an attitude of gratitude brings to every aspect of our lives, we will then begin to comprehend how just one negative thought can affect the whole and change the landscape of reality for everyone, as we are all connected and all one. So giving thanks and having gratitude can be a total game changer and can assist you in creating anything that you want, imagine, or are dreaming about; as there is nothing you cannot have, there is nothing you cannot do and there is nothing you cannot be. All you have to do is Believe in yourself and believe in your own power of co-creation. This is called "mindful intent", and it occurs when the imagination moves past the linear boundaries of restriction to embrace the possibility of everything. This is the force that literally drives the engine that facilitates every aspect of the Law of Abundance. Each aspect has the same face, wears the same expression, and achieves the same results. So it really doesn't matter which aspect you choose to embrace, as each will render you very similar outcomes depending upon the nature of your focus.

As you begin to use and hone these transformational tools and begin to incorporate them into your lives, windows of opportunity will start to appear for you ushering into your presence exactly what you were imagining and dreaming about. It is during these times that inspiration may come to you in the form of a new idea that suddenly pops into your head, seemingly out of nowhere, giving you exactly what you needed in order to accomplish your dreams. You may also be watching TV or listening to the radio and hear exactly what you needed to hear in order to shift your perspective and move you into a new direction, or a complete stranger may stop and talk to you and tell you something that begins to trigger a new idea to begin to form within your mind, causing your mind to expand outside the boundaries you put it in and move you in a direction that you had never even considered going. Pay attention, as the Universe is trying to give you what you need in order to accomplish your dreams. All of these new ideas are presenting themselves to you, for you to embrace. Honor them. They come from your "Higher Self" which is the highest aspect of who you truly are. Your higher self is the aspect of your spirit and soul that dwells within you as you. This aspect of yourself is connected to the universal source of all things. Listen closely, as when you do you might be totally astonished at how just one new thought has the capacity to open up the floodgates of abundance for you.

It is important during these times that you not second guess yourself and plant seeds of doubt within your mind telling yourself that you cannot accomplish any of this, or telling yourself to "give it up", as none of this is possible! Whenever that little nagging voice of doubt whispers in your ear "I can't do this" or "this will never work", begin to immediately replace that voice of doubt with a voice of hope saying to yourself "I absolutely Can Do this". Begin to see yourself as already having accomplished whatever it is that you have set out to do. Imagine in perfect detail just how happy you are that your ideas have taken root and have created for you everything you have ever dreamed about! This sets in motion the necessary vibrational shift needed to accomplish your dreams and to fulfill your visions. As you begin to see yourselves as having already received whatever it is you are imagining, a paradigm shift occurs within the very core of your being, ushering to you all the transformational energy needed to manifest those dreams into your realities. This then is the creational process behind every aspect of the Law of

Abundance, as whatever the mind thinks about and focuses on, it then creates. As such our worlds are driven and continually fueled by our thoughts. So honor those thoughts and use them wisely for they become your most powerful tool in creating your visions every second of every single day.

Embracing your lives with an attitude of gratitude creates a boomerang effect, as whatever you send out you get back in equal proportions. You see, as you send your thoughts out into the Universe they are received, transmitted and sent back to you reflecting to you whatever it is you were focusing upon. This embraces both the good as well as the bad as the universe is exact and doesn't discriminate between the two; it simply gives you whatever it is you want to experience. Therefore whenever you embrace a negative thought, try to be more cognizant of it, and slowly begin to replace those negative seeds with positive ones. This will shift your paradigm and alter your reality, moving in a more positive and abundant direction. This shift is what causes the tone within you to change and this is why it is so important that you be careful what you are focusing upon. For you see everything in creation is made up of pure undiluted energy; the Earth, Us, everything in the heavens and everything that dwells upon or within the Earth. We are all more deeply connected than you realize. Equally our thoughts and emotions are also made up of this same energy, which is why, by changing the direction of our thoughts to a more positive vibration, we are able to change the tone and the frequency of our vibrations and of our collective realities, changing the tone and frequency of what we then experience. This is how powerful each and every one of us is.

Every single person embraces within them a Universe within a Universe directly reflecting the order and wonder of creation within their own bodies. Just as every planet revolves around the sun so too does every molecule revolve around the nucleus of every cell within our bodies, directly reflecting the Hermetic Code of "As above So Below, As within So Without". Therefore "We" are each connected to "everything, everywhere." The energy that resides within the Sun is the same energy that resides within each of us. Therefore guarding our thoughts, which are the Architects of our realities, takes on a much different cadence when fully understood. The Law of Abundance and all connecting laws umbrellaed under it, are all tools we can use daily to create the fabric of our lives on a continuum. Every moment, whether we realize it or not, we are creating the infrastructure of our realities by the thoughts we hold within us. Now.... are you finally beginning to understand just how powerful your mind actually is and why it is so important to use your thoughts and emotions wisely in creating whatever it is you wish to experience?

This power source we collectively embrace as GOD, Yahweh, Allah, Buddha, the Source of all things, etc. created a field of energy that interconnects and embraces everything ...everywhere! This Source Field is always in motion, always in flux, always expanding and contracting with the In-breath and Outbreath of GOD. All Energy vibrates with Divine Frequency set to varying pathways of creation, from finer to denser, creating within the architecture of that creation what appears to be solid matter. Yet, nothing in creation is solid. Everything vibrates. Everything oscillates to a particular vibrational frequency uniquely its own, including us. Everything is movement; nothing is stationary. Solid matter is but an illusion of perception. This Law of Energy simply states that Energy of a certain vibration will attract Energy of a similar vibration, or in simpler terms; like will always attract like. Therefore the energy we radiate out from the cathedral of our minds will attract back to us the mirrored reflection of our thought process; bringing to us its exact counterpart. Our thoughts, Feelings and emotions have their own magnetic field held within the physical body. This magnetic field moves out of the seemingly solid structure of our beings, and carries our feelings and emotions out into the Universe to be received and filled. Once we begin to incorporate the Law of Abundance into our lives great changes begin to manifest for us, and as we begin to see the visible results of our efforts we will begin to realize that not only do we have the power to change our individual realities, but the realities of the entire planet as well. This is how powerful we all are, and when that power is trebled by many it begins to multiply exponentially, bringing more abundance and positive energy to everyone, everywhere. What affects anyone anywhere, affects everyone everywhere!

I have explained the Law of Abundance because it is important that this Law is understood in order to fully harness the powerful energy that exists within all of the prayers and mantras given within this book (as well as any prayer or mantra you are currently embracing). When you repeat out loud or in silence any prayer or mantra and do so with both focus and intent you create a pathway within you that has the potential to bring amazing changes into your life. This pathway creates a powerful frequency and vortex of light, which in turn activates the hidden powers held within each word that is spoken out loud or in silence. The words that create the prayers and mantras each vibrate to a particular frequency which is released into your presence as you voice and embrace them, and they bring with them transformational powers. Whether you believe in these powers or not, they exist, and are there for each of us to explore and embrace as well as to either accept or reject. Such is the power of free will. Yet rejecting this creational tool does not nullify its existence, it just closes your mind to the endless possibilities and potentials that it provides for you. The funny thing about this process is that even when the one saying these prayers and mantras has rejected the possibility of their powers they are still subtly bathed in the energy that is released when they are saying them. Whenever we speak a word or a phrase and do so with intent it brings back to us whatever emotional expression we have sent out. It doesn't matter whether that expression is positive or negative. It doesn't matter if it is something we have created within our minds or something we have read within a phrase. Whatever we reap we sow, whatever we think we create. Now guarding our thoughts takes on an entirely different meaning with consequences.

Within the following pages I have included Ancient Sanskrit and Kundalini Mantras as well as Mantras of Intent that I use every day. I have also included Mantras invoking the power of The I Am, as well as all of the Prayers contained within my first book that so many of you have been asking me to include. Many of these Mantras given within are not only powerful but ancient as well. When they are embraced they have the power to assist and guide you in your quest for truth and enlightment. Each Mantra and Prayer given has a specific vibrational tone and frequency expressing Divine Resonance. Every Mantra and Prayer is given to not only uplift and enlighten but to transform as well. Each has the capacity and power to expand the heart center creating a pathway leading to multidimensional awareness and quantum reality. This expansion of light has the power to accelerate the evolution of the soul. For you see Dear Ones, all Mantras and Prayers when spoken, chanted, or sung set in motion a resonance pattern with Divinity as they carry within them the vibrational frequency tones of the highly evolved Divine Masters and Avatars whose energy resides within the very structures they created.

In India there is a belief system that a "Mantra" is a creation of a series of sacred words which when repeated begins to create a shift of consciousness within. This shift creates a change of awareness bringing enlightenment and truth in its wake. For, as with all words the word "Mantra" contains within it the true meaning behind the word itself. The two syllables composing the word "Mantra" translate then as follows; Man=Mind and Tra=Liberation. Therefore a mantra when expressed in any manner liberates the mind of the one expressing it. It is interesting to denote that some of the world's most powerful Mantras originated within the Sanskrit language of India. This language is believed by many to be the "writings of the Gods" and as such it is believed to have existed since the beginning of time, as we know it. The Sanskrit collections of Mantras are indeed some of the oldest and most sacred texts known to mankind. They comprise sacred sounds that when spoken, chanted, or sung are considered capable of not only elevating and shifting your awareness and raising your consciousness, but of also effecting great changes within your biological structure. With their roots securely anchored in ancient India, Yogis and Adepts continually use these ancient mantras to help shift energy and elevate consciousness. Each Mantra given is associated with a unique tonal energy pattern that when repeated out loud or in silence, creates a very subtle energy shift within you that in turn raises your frequency vibration. This vibrational shift occurs because each word has its own vibrational tone that when spoken produces a corresponding effect within us. You see, words are sound and sound is vibration, and vibration produces and creates power, which generates both movement as well as resonance.

By repeating the following Mantras and prayers you will have the potential to tap into the endless source of love and abundance that flows throughout the Universe. When, as described earlier, these mantras are repeated and embraced with positive emotion, embracing gratitude, joy and happiness, they begin to retrain your brain's neural pathways, setting in motion a resonance pattern with the Universal Source of All Things. This process begins to change your body's vibrational frequency patterns, raising your own personal vibrations to a much higher band of consciousness, allowing you to not only recognize but to also receive all of the abundance the Universe has to offer. For you see, consciousness embraces everything! The understanding of the Laws of Quantum Physics has now crossed a major threshold proving that what we each perceive of as solid matter is actually nothing more or less than a vibrational energy frequency born out of consciousness, which is the purest substance in the Universe. When we embrace the higher consciousness of love and light, everything both seen and unseen is united into a pattern of harmonic resonance. Through embracing the following Mantras and Prayers, a higher pathway of consciousness can be achieved.

So I give to you these sacred words of wisdom in the form of both mantras and prayers in the hope that they will lead down the pathway of self-discovery and enlightenment, creating within you a shift of consciousness that unlocks the mysteries of the Heart. This journey you are embarking upon will be as unique as each and every one of you are. Each person's journey, having its own personal stamp of expression, and always remember Dear Ones; Every step of the journey "is" the journey.

# Sanskrit Mantras

## And

## Kundalini Yoga Mantras

"As her imagination took flight…
And her reality began to transform all around her…
She began to realize…
Just how powerful she really was…
And with that one realization…
Her World Changed forever"

The following Sanskrit Mantras originated from the spiritual work of the Yogis, which is why their impact is much more powerful when spoken in their original Sanskrit format. "Yoga" is the basis of all knowledge, as the meaning behind the word Yoga simply means the embracement of all Light and consciousness. It signifies everything in existence held within the circle of Now. It represents all that was, all that is, and all that will ever be.

1. This first Sanskrit Mantra is perhaps the simplest and yet one of the most powerful. It is the Mantra of

"OM"

This mantra emulates the original vibrational sound of the Universe. It represents both the in-breath as well as the out-breath of God and is believed to be the first original vibrational sound created, representing the endless infinite circle of Creation, Death, and rebirth, the perfect circle of life.

When this Mantra is spoken, it is phonetically pronounced as "AUM".

When taking a deep breath while saying the phrase "OM" and repetitively drawing that syllable out such as AUMMMMMMMMMM, between breaths, it centers us at the core of our being and brings us into perfect balance from within. By repetitively reciting the phrase "OM" it sets up a vibrational frequency pattern which then begins to alter and retrain the brain's neural pathways. This sets in motion a resonance pattern beginning in the Heart center, which then moves up through the brain to vibrate out through the top of the head. It is this vibrational frequency pattern that then moves out into the Universe to connect with the infinite Source of all things, and to the energy many refer to as GOD. This Resonance pattern then pushes out of the brain all dross and negative energies converting them to pure light energies. This is how powerful this simple Mantra is, but experiment with it to experience this power yourself. Begin by repeating the Mantra "OM" while placing your hand on the top of your head, and as you do so you will begin to feel the top of your head vibrating onto the palm of your hand. This vibration is the resonance pattern you have created simply by repeating the Mantra "OM". Now, how cool is that? There are many who believe that by repeating the Mantra of "OM" you will begin to create the pathway that will lead you to the true reality of existence, as this sacred Mantra connects you to the whole of creation and to the ever-expanding stream of divine consciousness. It is my favorite mantra!

2.The second Sanskrit Mantra is;

"OM Shanti…Shanti…Shanti OM"

This Mantra is referred to as the "Peace" Mantra and was created to envelop and embrace all that is and all that will ever be into arms of Peace. As this second Mantra is chanted or spoken we release the powerful frequency vibrations, which are held within each of the three consecutive Shantis. Each individual Shanti represents a particular element of our lives, which either brings us peace or blocks it, depending upon our intent.

The first of these three Shanti's is referred to as "Adhi-Daivikam" and represents all mental disturbances originating from God, or all things beyond our control, such as hurricanes, tornadoes, earthquakes, volcanic eruptions, tsunamis etc. So when we say this first Shanti we are praying to God to protect us from everything beyond our control.

The second Shanti is referred to as; "Adhi-Bhautikam". This second Shanti represents all disturbances that originate from the world around or within our environment, such as loud, angry, and abrasive noises from people yelling at each other, from fire engine or ambulance sirens, from screaming crowds and protesters, from loud music and even from swarms of pesky insects such as mosquitos or hornets. As opposed to the first Shanti that we have no control over, with this Shanti we actually do have some control. Here we can turn on the radio in our cars or shut the windows in our homes to drown out the sirens, call the authorities to handle the shouting and fighting, we can remove ourselves from the vicinity of the screaming crowds, and wear insect repellent to help protect us. So when we chant or say this second Shanti we are praying to God to protect us from not only our surrounding environment but to also protect us from all the negativity created by the people around us.

The third Shanti chanted or spoken is referred to as "Adhyatmikam". This Shanti represents all disturbances of inner peace we have created within ourselves and is the only one we have total and complete control over. This last Shanti is the most powerful of the three Shantis. This Shanti represents the pathway our minds take which is fueled by whatever our emotional state is at the time, both positive as well as negative. Keep in mind here that it is always our choice as to which of these emotions we will embrace! This last Shanti represents all of the disturbances created by our emotional and mental bodies, which are fueled and fanned continually by our Ego's need for total dominance and control. Here it is important to understand that the Ego is the only obstacle we ever need to overcome in order to achieve inner peace. If our inner realm represented by both our mental and emotional bodies is not calm, than neither will our physical bodies be, as the inner realm will always control the outer realm. Or in simpler terms, whatever we think and embrace we will then become. Having said that, the Ego will either stimulate within us compassion, tolerance and unconditional love; or the counterparts of resentment, anger, and hate. The trick here then, would be to try to balance the two opposing sides of ourselves represented by the two aspects of the Ego. Yet it is only when these two opposing aspects of ourselves are in complete balance that a state of inner peace can be obtained within. This is then the prize we each receive at the end of this amazing journey we have all chosen to embark upon when entering into this plane of existence. It is important to understand that both of these aspects of the Ego are very important for us to explore, as each teach us about our duality. It is through these lessons in duality that we each will have the opportunity to explore ourselves and through that exploration to finally have the opportunity to achieve inner peace. Once we achieve this inner balance there are no disturbances of any kind that will have the power to affect us.

As you are chanting or saying this Mantra it will be important for you to embrace an element of silence between each of the Shantis. This is important, as by pausing between saying each of the Shantis you are honoring and giving each of the individual aspects emphasis, while also offering up a respect for each of the three elements of peace contained and intertwined within this particular Mantra. This Mantra puts the emphasis on embracing peace both from within and without integrating both into one powerful expression of spiritual identity. Mirroring the "Hermetic Code" of, "As within so without; as above so below." When embraced, each individual aspect of this Mantra will express its own unique vibrational frequency interfacing all into one single and powerful vibration of peace.

3.The third Sanskrit Mantra given is


"OM Namah Shivaya".


This Mantra represents the highest and purest aspects of your higher self and literally translates to "I Bow to Shiva." Within the Sanskrit language "Shiva" is the supreme deity of transformation representing the purest aspect of the soul. This Mantra honors the divinity we each carry within us and brings to each of us the vibrational frequency energies of creation as it embraces all that is and all that will ever be. It serves to remind us that we are all created with divine energy and that we need to honor not only who we truly are, but to equally honor and respect the temple of our body, which houses our higher self and our soul. This Mantra reminds each of us that on a soul level we are absolutely connected to the Divine Source of all things, and that we can never be disconnected from that source. It teaches us, if we listen, that we are all a reflection of creation and that all of us carry within us this absolute divine truth.

The next few Mantras given are Kundalini Yoga Mantras

1. The first Kundalini Yoga Mantra given is;
"Sa Ta NA Ma"

This Mantra represents within Yoga Philosophy the five primal sounds of the universe and is referred to as a "Primal Awakening Mantra. These five primal sounds of expression are as follows; SSS, MMM, TTT, NNN and AAA. These primal sounds serve to awaken the Kundalini energy, which resides at the base of the spine moving it upwards through each of the chakras to in turn awaken the seat of consciousness that is held there. As each of our chakras begins the process of awakening it will begin to raise our consciousness into a much higher state of awareness. This is the pathway of ascension. This Kundalini energy has often been referred to as a "Serpent of Light" and is a spiritual snake-like current that rises upwards through our energy centers to awaken the third eye. When the third eye awakens and we connect with our higher self we then create within us a vibrational shift wherein the mind then expands out of its linear perception to tap into quantum reality. It is this vibrational shift that creates a pathway of expansion capable of plugging us into every aspect of creation. A word of caution here; this awakening of the Kundalini is a natural process and should never be forced, as if it is, it can short circuit your electrical system and damage the body. Just allow this flow of energy to move naturally during meditation as when it is left to its own rhythm it will always move in such a way as to be totally compatible with the body. The Mantra "Sa Ta Na Ma" is phonetically pronounced as "Saa Taa Naa Maa" and is considered to be a seed Mantra or Bij Mantra and is one of the most widely used Mantras within Kundalini yoga. It calls upon the infinite truth and wisdom of creation stored within our DNA and serves to awaken this truth and wisdom that exists within each of us. It is important here to understand that no one will ever be given more than they can handle at any given time. Each person's journey through this process of awakening will be unique and wholly their own, set to their own very personal pace and rhythm.

When embracing this powerful Mantra it is necessary that you understand the deep esoteric meanings that are contained within it as when this Kundalini phrase is spoken, chanted or sung it has the power to release into your presence all of the transformational energies that are stored within it. This transformational energy has the potential to affect you on many different levels of awareness depending upon the degree of enlightenment you are currently embracing.

This is so, as when you are verbalizing this Mantra you will have the power within you to bring into your presence all of the Universal mysteries of the infinite circle of life. Always keep in mind that you will never be given more than you can handle at any given time, so relax with it, and just let whatever wants to present itself to you just naturally happen, don't force the issue. Rest assured that your awakening within will always occur in such a manner that is totally appropriate for the enlightenment and Spiritual evolution of your soul. Thus, the meaning behind this Primal awakening Mantra can be described in the following manner; The letter "S" when pronounced will bring into your reality the powerful force of infinity, the letter "T" brings into your reality the powerful force of life, the letter "N " brings into your reality the powerful force of death, and the letter "M" brings into your reality the powerful force of rebirth and resurrection. When these 4 letters are combined with the vowel "A" pronounced as "AH" it increases and expands the powers held within each of the syllables by accelerating their vibrational tone. Within this Mantra the circle of life is both revered and honored. Like all Mantras the meaning behind this Mantra can be found within the entirety of the words. Here "Sat" represents the truth, while "Nam" represents the pathway or journey taken in order to awaken this knowledge stored within us and to awaken our "EQ" or "Emotional intelligence Quotient." Each of us has this stored within the DNA of every cell within our bodies. This "EQ" is just waiting to be put into action so that we can each move further up Jacob's ladder within our quest for spiritual enlightenment. Please note that when chanting or speaking a Mantra out loud the sounds we make can themselves be transformational. For instance, when we pronounce the vowel 'A' pronounced as 'AH' and use it within other words such as; Hallelujah or Amen; the sound expressed creates a transformational vibrational frequency that vibrates within our heart center having the power to clear out all negative and dross energies that are held there. But don't take my word for it, experiment with it yourselves. If you were to place your hand onto your heart while saying the syllable 'AH' you would actually begin to feel the vibration that this tone creates against the palm of your hand. Now how cool is that? So the vowel, "A" which incidentally is the first vowel, learned and expressed, is a very powerful accelerator of divine energy capable of uplifting and transforming all forms of expression held within its divine matrix.

2.  This next Kundalini Yoga Mantra is;
        "Sat Nam"


This Mantra translates to "truth is my identity." This powerful mantra reinforces the divine consciousness that resides within everyone and awakens it to merge with the whole of creation, intertwining all aspects of self with your divine birthright. This particular Mantra can also be used as a form of greeting as well as a Mantra. When this Kundalini Yoga Mantra is used as a greeting it embraces and acknowledges the Divinity in the one being greeted as it is given by one to the other as reverent form of respect, very similar to the Sanskrit word Namaste. When used as a Mantra it serves to awaken the Divine Consciousness that resides within each and every one of us. This amazing Mantra accomplishes this through the powerful vehicle of the breath, as when we are inhaling while saying the first syllable of this Mantra, "Sat", we are inhaling the truth of who we truly are, while when we are exhaling when saying the second syllable "Nam" we are exhaling our identity and releasing that identity out into the world to merge with the whole of creation. This mantra can help build concentration and mental focus, which in turn helps increase intuitive abilities within the one expressing it. In reality whenever we chant, sing, or verbalize this powerful mantra we are embracing the truest essence of who we are; Divine beings residing within the confinement of a wonderful yet seemingly limited vehicle of expression. This perceived limitation is but an illusion. All it takes to shatter this perceived illusion of confinement is for you to believe you can. This then begins to shift your perceptions to embrace unlimited nonlinear concepts held within the arms of Quantum reality. It is only through our inner realm of emotional and mental expression that we have the power to transcend mundane reality and let our spirits soar.

These two Kundalini Yoga mantras are considered the most fundamental and most important mantras in Kundalini Yoga. They are mantras for change and evolution and are often used to break addiction as they clear the system of all negativity.

# Mantras of Intent

"The Mind is everything. What you think you become"
*Buddha*

Mantras of Intent are very powerful vehicles and tools of transformation, as they serve to awaken the creative powers each of us has stored within us. Similar to the other Mantras given, when Mantras of Intent are verbally expressed they set up a frequency tone vibration that radiates out from our minds to connect with the creative stream of abundance that flows throughout the universe unobstructed, bringing back to us whatever it is we have focused on. A Mantra of Intent is essentially a statement of Divine Intent, which produces through the expression of sound a vibration that pulsates at a rate within the one expressing it, and is completely in tune with the energy vibration of the Mantra itself. These Mantras can be used as tools that, when invoked, become the key that unlocks the creative powers of the universe. Once unlocked, our creative powers enable us to recreate our realities instantly. Deepak Chopra once stated; "Our destiny is ultimately shaped by our deepest intentions and desires. An intention is a directed impulse of consciousness that contains the seed form of that which you aim to create. Like real seeds intentions can't grow if you hold onto them. Only when you release your intentions into the fertile depths of your consciousness can they grow and flourish." Intentions move out from the fertile soil of our minds into the Universe to be fulfilled through the frequency tone of our thoughts. When we put those thoughts into motion through the powerful vehicle of the mind and release them to be embraced by the Laws of Abundance we need to always remember to infuse those thoughts with an attitude of gratitude and absolute trust that they have been received and will manifest for us. Try not to put limitations on your dreams but rather let your dreams become the framework that your thoughts can then build upon. After you state your intention either internally or verbally, let it go, try not to worry about it being received and fulfilled as the Universe has amazing organizing powers and will receive your request and send back to you exactly what you have asked for. There is a saying that "you are the sum total of your beliefs" or to put a different spin on it, "your psychology becomes your biology". So through the constant focus of your thoughts you have the power within you to either bring balance or chaos into your life, it is all a matter of perspective. That is how powerful the mind is.

The following is a simple equation that explains the pathway of synergy between the focus of your thoughts and the tone of your intent interfacing with the frequency and hue of your emotions;

$$\text{"I AM = I Intend"}$$

Now how simple is that? Who you are and what you think are one and the same. One aspect of you creates while the other aspect of you receives, all the while remaining whole.

The following are Mantras of Intent that I have found to be very powerful vehicles of manifestation. These Mantras all begin with... "I Intend"... after which you fill in whatever it is you are intending to manifest into reality.

For example; "I Intend... to be very successful at everything I set out to do".

This is just one of many different combinations of wordings you can use within these Mantras of Intention. This particular formula of success can literally be tailor-made to suit each individual person who is embracing it. The sky's the limit, so to speak, as there is absolutely nothing you cannot ask for. So don't limit yourselves. Be creative and play around with this and watch magic occur for you right before your eyes, as what you have expressed as your intention of creation suddenly becomes your reality.

The following are examples of intentions you can use daily to alter the course of your reality and bring abundance to you;

1. I intend that all of my needs of food, shelter and grooming have now been met with great financial abundance, with plenty left over so I can pursue all of my dreams.

2. I intend to exceed every goal I set for myself and to constantly challenge myself to create new ones.

3. I intend that my body has now totally regenerated and rejuvenated itself, has reversed all signs of aging and is now in perfect radiant health and well-being.

4. I intend to always try to see the good in others.

5. I Intend to Be the Change I wish to see in the World.

6. I intend to embrace an attitude of gratitude as soon as I wake up every morning, therefore setting a positive tone for each new day

7. I intend that every paycheck I bring home exceeds $_____
        *(You fill in the blank here)*

8. I intend to always be kind and to always have compassion for those who are less fortunate than I am.

9. I intend to always expand my mind to new possibilities, and in doing so, to open myself up to new ideas and concepts, allowing me to grow past my previous limitations.

10. I intend to embrace my inner child, to laugh and to dance with abandonment and to begin to see the world through the eyes of wonder and awe.

11. I intend to honor the planet by treating her with respect and reverence.

12. I intend to plant a garden so that I can become more self-sufficient and at the same time create a space where I now show respect for Mother Earth

13. I intend to create enough wealth in my life so that there is enough left over to feed the homeless.

14. I Intend to embrace a positive can-do attitude where anything is possible and everything is probable.

15. I intend to be the light in the darkness so those who are lost can find their way home again.

16. I intend to meditate for at least 15 minutes every day and to learn to control the breath so that I am now in perfect synchronistic harmony and at one with everything.

17. I intend to try not to take criticism personally but to rather look at it as a way to expand and grow.

18. I intend to focus only on thoughts that bear the light, therefore helping to uplift the

vibrations of the entire planet.

19. I intend to never put my happiness in someone else's hands but to rather take control over my own life and to be responsible for my own happiness.

20. I intend to embrace the knowledge that very often kindness is more important than wisdom. I shall do one act of kindness every single day to help uplift the planet.

Prayers from *Believe,*
*A Journey of Enlightenment*

Everything is energy and that's all there is to it.

Match the frequency of the reality you want and
You cannot help but get that reality.

It can be no other way.

This is NOT philosophy.

This IS physics."

*Albert Einstein*

The following prayers are from my first book *Believe, A Journey of Enlightenment*" and are given with very few modifications from their original format. A few have been slightly modified for better flow and clarification. All are given to assist any who choose to embrace them as tools for transformation and for spiritual evolution. They are as follows:

A. Prayer to balance and expand the Chakra system;

"I give thanks to the Universal Spirit and source of all things for providing me with a perfect body through which I can experience life to its fullest.

I call upon the Spirit and the Source of all things to aid and assist me in bringing into perfect balance all seven of my Chakras, as well as both my gross anatomy and subtle anatomy comprising of; my physical body, my emotional body, my mental body and my spiritual body; until all are vibrating in perfect harmony with all that is and all that will ever be and are now aligned within the light of creation.

I ask that the light of creation awaken and expand each seat of consciousness held within every one of my energy centers so that they are now in perfect alignment with the energies of both love and compassion and are in total balance and harmony with the light.

I do this with an attitude of gratitude that Spirit has answered my every call.

Thank you Mother/Father GOD it is done.

B. Prayer to invoke the Elohim of Creation;

"I call upon GOD,and the Elohim of Creation, to come into my presence and free me from all of the negative baggage I have embraced and created in not only this lifetime, but in all other lifetimes as well, both known and unknown. I ask that you lift me up into the light of compassion, unconditional love and understanding so that my entire being is now free of all negative emotion. I ask that you move through me and become one with me and in the process that you awaken my divinity. I ask that you bestow upon me the Divine Power to change my world in an instant to one of love, peace, hope, compassion, harmony and abundant co-creation wherein all are then transformed into the love and grace of GOD. I ask that you help me to remember who I am and to assist me in bringing myself back into alignment with the true spiritual being I have always been.
I ask that you shine this Divine light into my presence so that I will remember what was, embrace what now is and will now have the power to co-create with you what will be.
I send this all back with Divine Love. Thank you Mother/Father GOD it is done."


C. Prayer to invoke the Cobalt Blue Flame of Protection into my presence;

"I call upon the Archangel Michael to come into my presence and ask him to, with his sword, bring out from the mind of GOD the Cobalt Blue Flame of Protection and send it spinning down into my being so that it permeates every cell, every molecule, and every quark in my body so that I am now held within the complete protection of this living color of GOD and am now invisible, invincible, and invulnerable to anything and everything except the Divine protection of GOD.

I send this back with divine love. Thank you Mother /Father GOD it is done"

D. Prayer to invoke the Violet Consuming Flame of Transmutation into my presence;

"I call upon Saint Germaine, the Archangel Michael, the mighty Angel from Venus "Victory", Jesus the Cosmic Ascended Christ, the Archangel Zadkiel who works only with the violet consuming flame, and Omri Tos, who is the ruler of the violet planet; which is the secret love star of the bible, a 5th dimensional planet dwelling upon the etheric plane of existence. I ask that these Divine Beings send the Violet consuming flame spinning into my presence until it permeates through every cell, atom and quark within my body, and with this flame to consume and purify all human suffering that I have ever created in any time frame, in any dimension, in any universe both known or unknown.

I ask these Divine Beings to blaze, consume, and purify the cause, the effect, the record and the memory of all human negativity I have ever created within my physical body, my emotional body, my mental body and my spiritual body until all four of my bodies are lifted up into the consciousness of love, light, peace and harmony so that I am now truly able to be of service according to Divine Will, for Divine purpose, and according to my Divine plan. I am now validated and I am now that Violet Consuming flame in action here in its most powerful dynamic expression of love, freedom, and purification.

I send this all back with an attitude of gratitude
Thank you Mother/Father GOD it is done."

E.) Prayer of both protection and transmutation.

(Within this prayer feel free to substitute whatever it is you personally wish to protect and change. The prayer that follows is an example of the prayer I use);

"In the name of Mother/Father God whose power is greater then any power on earth or in heaven I ask that my aura, my husband's aura, Venus's aura, our home, our property, our automobiles, our bank accounts, our identities, our investments, our abundance, and the auras of all of our family and friends be sealed within triple cones of golden white light. I ask that this golden white light be infused with the violet consuming flame of transmutation and surrounded with the cobalt blue flame of protection. I ask that everything and everyone be surrounded with a mirror like substance so that anything of a negative nature is directed back to its source. I send this back with an attitude of gratitude that Spirit has answered my every call.

"Thank you Mother/Father God it is done."

F. The Universal Lord's Prayer known as The Our Father;

"Our Father who art in Heaven
Hallowed be thy name.
Thy Kingdome come
Thy will be done, on Earth as it is in Heaven.
Give us this day our daily bread and
Forgive us our debts as we forgive our debtors and
Lead us not into temptation, but deliver us from evil.
For thine is the Kingdom, the power and the glory
Of the Father, the Son, and the Holy Spirit forever and ever. Amen"

G.) Prayer to invoke the power of the I Am into your presence;

(It is important to denote that when "I Am" is attached to any word it will invoke very strong connotations of that word. When we put "I am", which is at the same time both a noun and a verb before any word, we bring into our presence the vibrational tone of the words we are speaking. For example; when we state "I Am beautiful" it is equally as powerful as the statement "I Am ugly". This is why it is so important to guard your word wisely as they have the power to both uplift as well as destroy. This is one of the secrets hidden within all spoken languages.)

"I thank the Universal Spirit of all that is for this day and I choose to see only light, love, and innocence within myself and others.
I invite the presence of that Spirit into every situation.

I choose to be all that I Am and to know that it is safe to honor and cherish my true identity.
I am a spiritual being in a physical body.
I am love, loved, loving, and lovable.
I am a beautiful, desirable and empowered person.
I know that true prosperity is perfect health, wealth and happiness.
I accept that Spirit is the source of all supply and that money is Spirit in action.
Love is flowing from me and to me so richly and so fully that I now have abundance, prosperity and affluence to share and to spare today and always.
My body regenerates itself and I emanate perfect health.
I Am breathing fully and vibrantly today and always.
I choose to give up all difficulty and to be a living example of human potential.
These words I speak in faith as they activate a law of Universal good and I accept and share the results.
I am grateful for these blessings, for the increase in them and for all others knowing that we prosper together in every way."

"I am rich in my heart.
I am rich in my soul.
I am rich in my life.
I am rich and I am whole.
Thank you for blessing me."
        (Author Unknown)


H. Here I have broken up the above prayer into separate mantras for you to use to invoke the powerful vibrational tone of the "I AM" into your presence. This vibrational tone is totally compatible with the vibrational tone of the "I Intend" mantras given earlier and both will produce for you the same results.

1) I am a spiritual being residing within a physical body and I invite the presence of spirit into every situation.

2) I choose to be all that I am and to know that it is safe to honor and cherish my true identity.

3) I am a Spiritual being in a physical body, I am love, loved, loving and lovable.

4) I am a beautiful/handsome, desirable and empowered person.

5) I am a divine being and I know that true prosperity is perfect health, wealth and happiness and I consciously choose to embrace all three.

6) I am divinity in action and I accept that Spirit is the true source of all abundance and that money is simply Spirit in action.

7) I am a being of love and I radiate that love outward so richly and fully that I now have an endless supply of abundance, prosperity and affluence to share and spare today and always.

8) I am in perfect radiant health and well-being and my body regenerates itself continually.

9) I am empowered and I have totally learned to control my breath through meditation and prayer and have now changed my molecular structure to one of perfect balance and harmony.

10) I am inspired and in that inspiration I choose to give up all difficulty and become a living example of perfect human potential.
11) I am rich in my heart, I am rich in my soul, I am rich in my life, I am rich and I am whole."


I. Prayer to open and expand the third eye of abundant co-creation

(You can activate this synergy of spirit through meditation and prayer and within this process open up the third eye of expansion through the following prayer);


"I give thanks to the Universal Spirit and source of all things and feel this divine energy fill my entire being with love, light and wisdom. As I embrace these Divine properties I feel them permeate every cell, atom, molecule, and quark within my body until they have brought my entire being into perfect balance and harmony. I invoke the power of the holy trinity to awaken the light within me so I am now vibrating in perfect unison with all that is and all that will ever be. I feel this light moving up through my chakras to activate and interface with my magnetic field, held within my third eye, uplifting and changing the vibrational tone that my dreams travel upon and aligning me within every aspect of creation.
I feel this light radiating outward from the center of my brow connecting me to everything everywhere and as I feel this connection I release all preconceived

notions of separateness seeing the world around me through the eyes of unconditional love and unity. I now have the absolute power to manifest anything and everything I can imagine bringing into my reality whatever it is I desire to create and experience knowing beyond knowing whatever my focus is I will then become.

I send this back with an attitude of gratitude that spirit has answered my every call.

Thank you Mother/Father God it is done."


J. Magical Prayer
From beneath me arises the energy of the Earth; my home and my foundation.
From above me pours the light of the Sun and the enchanting moon.
To my right hand flows the strength to control and direct the power of Magic.
To my left hand comes the skill to divine and to heal, the source of all blessings."

(Author unknown)
Source: Magical School

# Conclusion

Dear Reader,

I challenge you to embrace the breathing techniques within this book and make them your own.

I encourage you to use both the mantras and prayers given as tools to activate the light within you. These varying tools that are given have the power to invoke the Laws of Abundance into your presence, altering your realities into any reality you could ever imagine.

The sky's the limit, so try to not put limitations on your dreams. Rather, imagine them, create them, set them free, and then let them soar.

Imagine the endless possibilities and potentials you have stored deep within you, which you can activate at any time simply by embracing your inner power!

This journey into self-discovery that we are all embarked upon is a journey of revelations. It is a journey once taken that removes the blinders of ignorance from our collective eyes. As we begin the process of peeling away the misperceptions we have embraced for a lifetime, and begin to replace them with a new awareness of who we actually are and who it is possible for each and every one of us to become.

Our parameters begin to shift and a new reality subtly begins to replace the matrix and foundation of the old one. We are the Architects of our worlds and are totally responsible for what we each embrace and experience.

This is a journey that will teach us, if we let it, that we can accomplish anything that we can imagine simply by embracing positive thoughts and infusing those thoughts with emotion, intent and focus. This journey can bring many changes into your lives, but it will ultimately be what you choose to believe as your inner truth that will set you free.

*Namaste*

Made in the USA
Middletown, DE
14 January 2018